MY BODY SAFETY RULES

Educating and empowering children with disability about body boundaries, consent and body safety skills

Note to Parents, Caregivers, Educators and Healthcare Professionals

This book aims to teach children with disability about body safety and consent, and provide them with essential skills to recognize unsafe situations. Using age-appropriate language and illustrations, this book addresses the needs and challenges often faced by children with disability, helping them to understand their rights in regard to their body and personal space.

This book serves two purposes. The first is to educate your child in body safety and consent, and what they can expect from the people who interact with them; and secondly to educate family, caregivers, teachers and healthcare professionals in the concepts of body safety and the language of consent, and how they need to respect your child's rights especially in regard to their body.

This book may be read over a number of sittings, depending on your child's needs. Please take the time to discuss each rule, the illustrations and engage your child in the questions provided. These important conversations are ongoing and should continue in daily interactions with your child and your child's caregivers. There are in-depth Discussion Questions on pages 36-38 to further draw out the learning.

Each child's disability is unique. Please adapt the text to the needs and abilities of your child, for example, children who are non-verbal will need to show other ways such as using body language or communication devices to indicate their needs.

Thank you for taking this journey with your child. Your efforts in teaching them about body safety and consent are invaluable.

Jayneen

My Body Safety Rules
Educate2Empower Publishing an imprint of
UpLoad Publishing Pty Ltd
Victoria Australia
www.upload.com.au

This edition first published in 2024
Text copyright © Jayneen Sanders 2024
Illustration copyright © UpLoad Publishing Pty Ltd 2024

Written by Jayneen Sanders
Illustrations by Farimah Khavarinezhad

Jayneen Sanders asserts her right to be identified as the author of this work.
Farimah Khavarinezhad asserts her right to be identified as the illustrator of this work.

Designed by Stephanie Spartels, Studio Spartels

*Many thanks to 'Children and Young People with Disability Australia' (CYDA)
for their invaluable advice and support. J.S.*

ISBN: 9781761160462 (hbk) 9781761160455 (pbk)

A catalogue record for this book is available from the National Library of Australia

Disclaimer: The information in this book is advice only written by the author based on her advocacy in this area, and her experience working with children as a classroom teacher and mother. The information is not meant to be a substitute for professional services or advice. For professional help if you are concerned about a child's behavior, go to a health professional and/or contact the key organizations listed at www.e2epublishing.info/links

MY BODY! MY RULES!

Hi! I'm Eli. In this book you will learn **7 Body Safety Rules** to help keep you safe. You have rights -- especially around your body. Rights are rules that all people need to follow.

This book will help you learn about your right to be safe so if you ever feel unsafe, uncomfortable or worried, you can get the help you need.

Please share this book with your family, caregivers, teachers and healthcare workers.

THIS IS MY BODY!

My body may look and work differently from yours but it's **my** body! And I have rules about my body.

Everyone -- young or old -- needs to follow my rules when they...

MY BODY! MY RULES!

help me

teach me

play games with me

or look after me.

I use a wheelchair to get around. Your abilities might be very different from mine but the **7 Body Safety Rules** you will learn in this book are the same for you and for me.

These rules need to be followed at school, at home, the swimming pool, the library, the hospital -- anywhere YOU go!

RULE 1:
ASKING FOR CONSENT

People need to ask for my **consent** before they enter my **body boundary.** My body boundary is the invisible space around my body and my wheelchair. It's my personal space -- a space just for me.

MY BODY BOUNDARY MAY BE INVISIBLE BUT IT'S STILL THERE!

Body boundary

Everyone has a body boundary: babies, children, teenagers and adults too!

Consent is an important word. It means asking if something is okay or not okay. It means one person asks for permission and the other person gives permission.

When my caregiver, Josie, needs to push my wheelchair or help me from my chair -- she needs to **ask** me first. Josie is asking for my consent.

If I say 'no' or 'I'm not ready yet', then Josie needs to listen to me and wait until I say I am ready.

If I happily say 'yes', then Josie can lift me out of my chair and onto my bed. Yay!

CAN I LIFT YOU NOW?

YES!

Giving consent

REMEMBER!
Rule 1 Asking for Consent also needs to happen if you are being helped into a car, train or an aeroplane; when someone helps you to brush your teeth, wash your body or get dressed. People always needs to ask for your consent before they enter your body boundary.

→ IF YOU CAN'T SAY THE WORDS, WHAT ARE SOME OTHER WAYS YOU CAN SHOW A VERY HAPPY 'YES'?

→ WHO ARE YOUR CAREGIVERS? DO THEY ASK FOR YOUR CONSENT WHEN THEY MOVE YOUR BODY?

*This rule applies to family members, caregivers, teachers and all healthcare professionals.

And even if I have said 'yes' to Josie lifting me out of my chair, she needs to keep **checking in** with me. This is to make sure I have not changed my mind, or I'm uncomfortable.

She might say things like, 'Would you like to lie down now? May I lift your leg? Can I cover you with a blanket? Is everything okay?'

CAN I COVER YOU WITH A BLANKET?

Checking in

YES, PLEASE!

What Josie is doing when she asks for my **consent**, and she keeps **checking in**, is showing me **respect**. Respect is another important word. It means you understand another person's wishes, you check with them, and you care about them and their wishes.

Josie always listens to me and gives me time to answer. Sometimes I need a minute or two to think, then answer. And that's okay!

→ DO YOUR CAREGIVERS CHECK IN WITH YOU? WHAT SORT OF THINGS DO THEY SAY?

*This rule applies to family members, caregivers, teachers and all healthcare professionals.

RULE 3:
GREETINGS ARE MY CHOICE

It's always my choice how I greet people. People should never hug or kiss me without asking me first. They need to ask for my consent. And they need to listen and wait for my reply.

When my Uncle Kip asks me for a hug, I can choose to say 'yes' or 'no'. It's up to me and only me.

CAN I HAVE A HUG?

YES!

Remember!
Everyone has a body boundary. So you also need to ask for a person's consent before you hug or kiss them, or enter their body boundary. You need to ask if they are okay with a hug or a kiss. If they are silent or say, 'no, thanks' or 'I'm not sure' you need to listen to this and not hug or kiss them. If they say a very happy 'yes!' then you can give them a hug or a kiss.

Sometimes I might say 'yes' and sometimes I might say 'no'. And just because I said 'yes' to a hug or kiss last week, doesn't mean I have said 'yes' to a hug or kiss this week. People need to ask me how I would like to be greeted every time.

Josie always asks, 'How would you like me to greet you today?'

Sometimes I say I'd like a hug, but I always ask if she's okay with that. And sometimes I say I'd like a high-five, a fist bump or a handshake. We **all** have choices in how we greet people.

HOW WOULD YOU LIKE ME TO GREET YOU TODAY?

→ WHAT IS YOUR FAVORITE WAY TO GREET PEOPLE?

*This rule applies to family members, caregivers, teachers and all healthcare professionals.

RULE 4:
PRIVATE AND PUBLIC SPACES

Private means just for me. A private space might be my bedroom or bathroom.

Public spaces are places everyone uses such as the kitchen or a classroom.

When I'm in my bedroom or the bathroom, people need to ask for my **consent** (or permission) to enter this space. They need to knock and ask if they can come in. And they need to listen and wait for my reply.

I need help to go to the bathroom and I need help to get dressed and undressed -- **but** RULE 1 ASKING FOR CONSENT and RULE 2 CHECKING IN still need to happen in these situations.

→ WHAT ARE THE PRIVATE SPACES IN YOUR HOUSE? WHAT IS YOUR FAVORITE PUBLIC SPACE?

*This rule applies to family members, caregivers, teachers and all healthcare professionals.

RULE 5:
PRIVATE PARTS ARE PRIVATE

We all have private parts. These are the parts of our body under our bathing suit or underwear.

Most boys have a penis, testicles and a bottom.

Most girls have a vulva on the outside and a vagina on the inside. They also have nipples and a bottom. When girls get older the area around their nipples grow into breasts.

A person's bottom is also known as their buttocks.

These are the correct names for our private parts. We should always use the correct names for our private parts and so should our family members, caregivers, teachers and healthcare workers.

Our Bodies

If I'm alone in a private space, it's okay for me to touch my own private parts. This is absolutely okay.

But it's NOT okay for a family member, caregiver, teacher or healthcare worker to touch my private parts without a very good reason such as when a private part hurts or I have an injury.

As well as having a very good reason, there are two more things they need to do:

1. ask for my consent and

2. make sure one of my safe adults is in the room.

Josie is one of my safe adults -- I trust her. Josie needs to wash and dry my private parts because I can't do this by myself. And that's okay. But, RULE 1 ASKING FOR CONSENT and RULE 2 CHECKING IN **always** need to happen in these situations.

→ WHAT DO YOU THINK 'TRUST' MEANS? WHO ARE YOUR SAFE ADULTS? WHY ARE THEY YOUR SAFE ADULTS?

Josie needs to ask for my consent before washing or drying my private parts, and she needs to listen and wait for my answer. She also needs to keep checking in with me to see if I'm still okay.

Having Josie wash and dry my private parts can sometimes be uncomfortable. But I can say 'stop' at anytime and I know Josie will stop straightaway. I am learning to wash and dry my own private parts so I don't always need Josie's or one of my parents' help.

Josie listens to and respects my voice at all times. She is a very respectful caregiver.

→ HOW DO YOU SHOW OR SAY TO A PERSON THAT YOU ARE UNCOMFORTABLE OR YOU DON'T FEEL SAFE?

When Josie or my parents have to wash or clean my private parts, they always ask for my consent first.

ELI! IS IT OKAY IF I WASH YOUR PRIVATE PARTS?

NO, THANKS. I CAN WASH MY OWN PRIVATE PARTS TODAY.

My mouth is also a private part or private zone, so Josie and my parents use RULE 1 ASKING FOR CONSENT and RULE 2 CHECKING IN if they or a dentist need to clean my teeth or look inside my mouth.

DOES YOUR DENTIST ASK FIRST BEFORE LOOKING INSIDE YOUR MOUTH? WHAT CAN YOU DO IF THEY DON'T ASK FOR YOUR CONSENT?

*This rule applies to family members, caregivers, teachers and all healthcare professionals.

RULE 6:
FEELING SAFE AND UNSAFE

Caregivers, teachers and healthcare workers all need to make you feel safe when they are with you. If you don't feel safe, your body is very smart and it will let you know. You might get a sick feeling in your tummy or your heart might beat really fast. These feelings in your body are called your Early Warning Signs.

Other Early Warning Signs you may get are:

HAIR FEELS LIKE IT IS STANDING ON END

SWEATY BROW

STARTS TO CRY

GOOSEBUMPS

HEART BEATS FAST

SHAKY ALL OVER

FEELS SICK IN THE TUMMY

SWEATY PALMS

NEEDS TO GO TO THE TOILET

WOBBLY LEGS

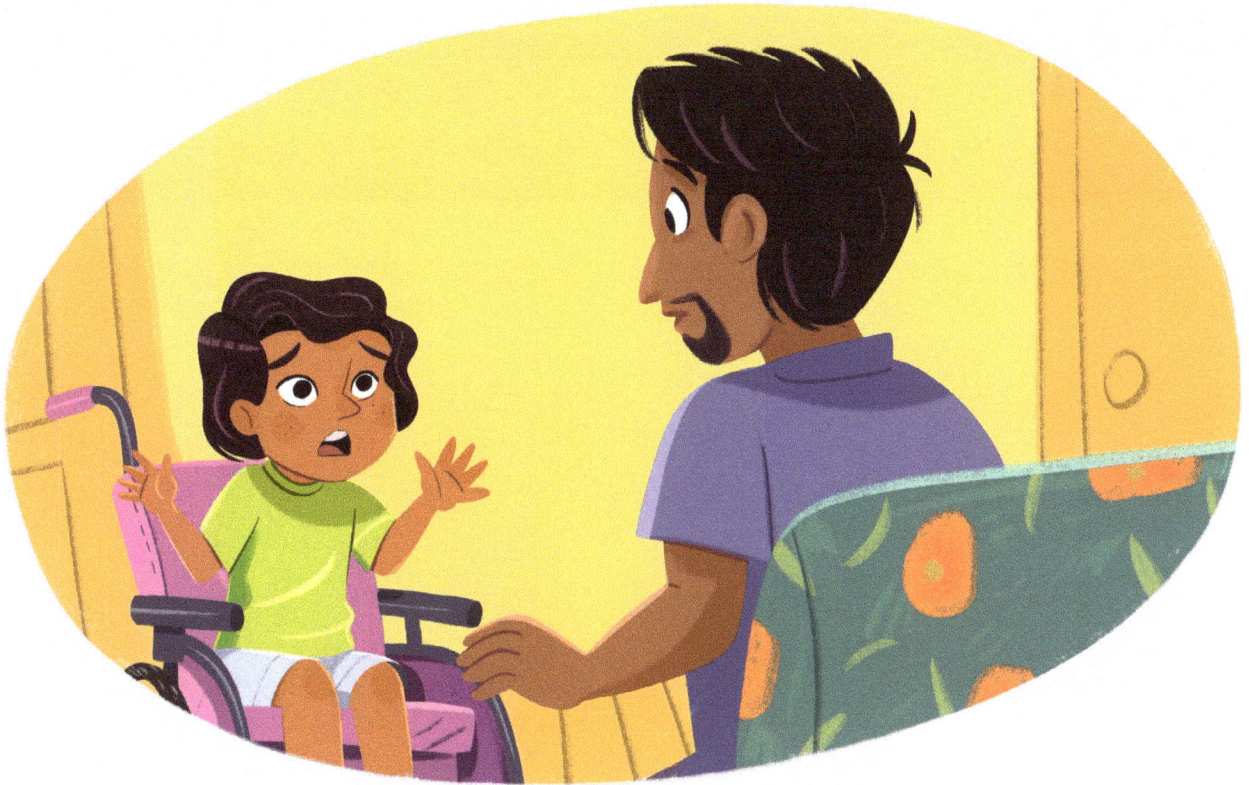

If **any** of these feelings happen -- you need to tell your safe adult. A safe and trusted adult is a grown-up who:

→ cares for you very much

→ makes you feel safe

→ always listens to you

→ will always believe you when you say you are feeling worried or unsafe

→ will help you.

→ WHO ARE 3 TRUSTED ADULTS THAT MAKE YOU FEEL SAFE?

It's a good idea for you to choose 3 to 5 of these safe adults to be on your **Safety Network**. A Safety Network is a group of trusted adults who will always help you if you feel worried, uncomfortable or unsafe. One person should not be a member of your family.

I FEEL SAFE. I HAVE A SAFETY NETWORK!

MAMA

DAD

MR LONG (MY TEACHER)

JOSIE

Remember! Who you choose to be on your Safety Network is always YOUR choice.

Draw around your hand to make an outline.
Now write each person's name on your Safety Network hand.
Display this in your house or classroom so other people know
who is on your Safety Network.

MAMA
DAD
MR LONG
JOSIE

MY SAFETY
NETWORK

WHERE WILL YOU
DISPLAY YOUR SAFETY
NETWORK HAND?

Things that might make you feel **unsafe** are:

→ being yelled at or hit

→ not being listened to

→ being spoken to in an unkind or disrespectful way

→ someone teasing you or making fun of you

→ someone entering your body boundary without asking for your consent

→ someone touching your body in an unsafe way

→ someone touching your private parts in an unsafe way

→ someone wanting to photograph your private parts or asking you to photograph your private parts and share these pictures.

Here's what you need to do if any of these things happen.

1. Only if it's safe to do so, say in a loud voice,
'Stop! This is my body!' or **'Stop! I don't like that!'**

STOP! I DON'T LIKE THAT!

2. Tell a safe adult on your Safety Network about who and what made you feel unsafe as soon as you can.

3. If they do not listen, tell the next adult on your Safety Network. Keep telling other adults on your Safety Network until one of them believes you and helps you.

4. And please remember, if someone makes you feel unsafe or touches you in an unsafe way it is **never ever** your fault.

→ IF YOU CAN'T SAY THE WORDS, HOW MIGHT YOU SHOW A SAFE ADULT THAT YOU FEEL UNSAFE?

If someone asks you to touch or look at their private parts or shows you pictures of private parts:

1. Tell a safe adult on your Safety Network as soon as you can.

2. If they do not listen, tell the next adult on your Safety Network. Keep telling other adults on your Safety Network until one of them believes you and helps you.

3. And please remember, if someone makes you feel unsafe or touches you in an unsafe way it is **never ever** your fault.

Remember!
It is never too late to tell a trusted adult what has happened and how you are feeling.

→ IS THERE ANYONE
OR ANYTHING ELSE THAT
MAKES YOU FEEL UNSAFE?

RULE 7: DON'T KEEP SECRETS

If someone asks me to keep a secret or says, 'Don't tell anyone! It's our little secret.' -- this is **not** okay. So, I say:

I DON'T KEEP SECRETS, ONLY HAPPY SURPRISES BECAUSE THEY WILL ALWAYS BE TOLD.

Secrets can make you feel bad, especially if the person says you must never tell. That's why in my family and my community we don't have secrets. We only have happy surprises that will eventually be told -- like not telling Mama about her surprise birthday party.

SURPRISE!

SURPRISE!

SURPRISE!

If someone asks you to keep an unsafe secret like touching your private parts, kissing or showing you pictures of private parts, tell an adult on your Safety Network **as soon as you can**.

Secrets like those should be told. And even if the person tells you not to tell -- secrets like those need to be told.

Everyone is different.

My body may be different from your body.

And my abilities may be different too. And that's okay!

But what is the same is our right to feel safe, loved, healthy and happy.

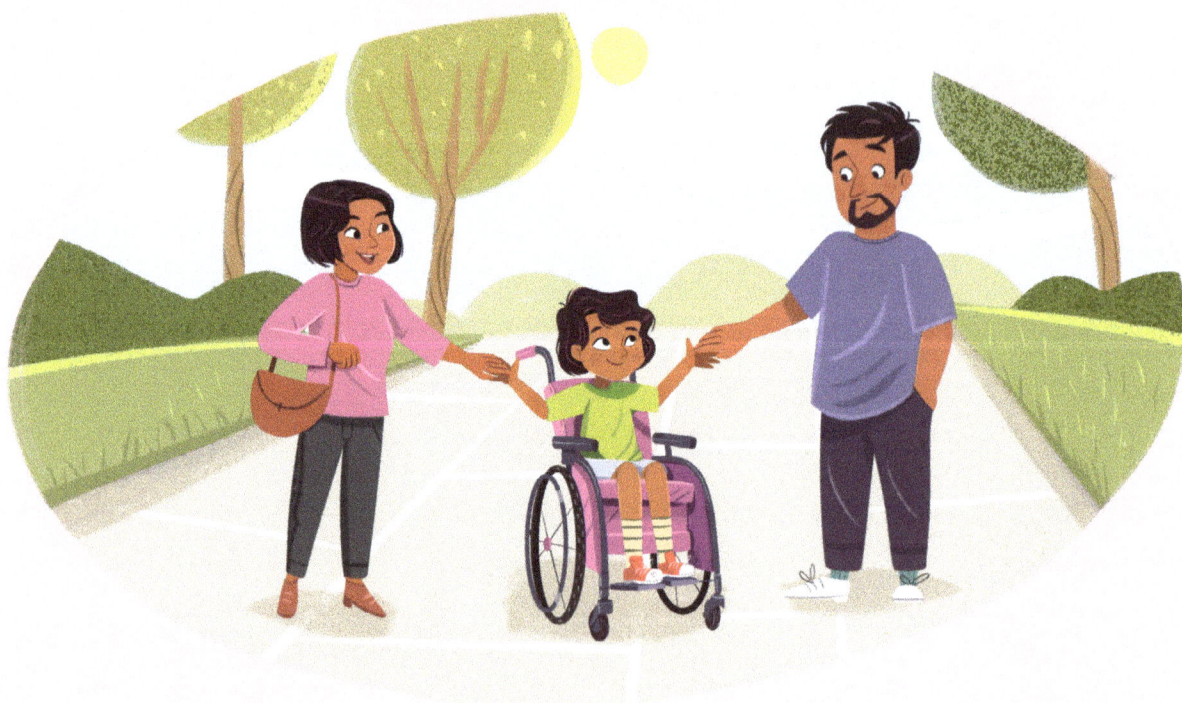

Knowing these **7 Body Safety Rules** will help to keep you safe in two ways:

1. You will know your rights around your body and what to do if you feel unsafe.

2. By sharing this book with your family, caregivers, teachers and healthcare workers they will be aware of your rights and how you expect to be treated.

It's a win for all!

MY BODY! MY RULES!

1. Asking for Consent

2. Checking In

3. Greetings Are My Choice

4. Private and Public Spaces

5. Private Parts Are Private

6. Feeling Safe and Unsafe

7. Don't Keep Secrets

DISCUSSION QUESTIONS
for Parents, Caregivers, Educators and Healthcare Professionals

The following Discussion Questions are intended as a guide and can be used to initiate open and empowering dialogues with your child around personal body safety, feelings, safe and unsafe touch, private parts, secrets and surprises, consent and respectful relationships. The questions are optional and/or can be explored at different readings. I suggest you allow your child time to answer the questions both on the internal pages and in this section, as well encourage them to ask their own questions around this very important topic. It is equally important that you value their input and listen to their voice. All of these discussions will help increase your child's skills and knowledge around personal body safety and consent, and will boost their confidence and empowerment. Remain calm and confident discussing this topic with your child as they will take their cues from you. Praise your child's responses and always reassure them. Finally, it is an adult's responsibility to educate themselves around child sexual abuse and the grooming that can occur (see *Body Safety Education: a parent's guide to protecting kids from sexual abuse*). That way, as the child's 'safe person,' you are proactive in helping to keep them safe. It is not the child's responsibility but ours, as adults.

Pages 4-5

Have a general discussion around the fact that all bodies are different and that's okay, and that each person is unique with unique challenges and unique abilities. Ask, 'Do you have any specific rules people need to follow?' Reinforce that the rules your child is about to learn need to be followed by all people in all situations, for example, at school, in a taxi, on a plane, at the hospital, at the swimming pool, etc.

Pages 6-7

Have you and your child outline your own invisible body boundary. Explain that this is their personal space and they can decide who enters it. Unpack consent by providing examples. For example, you could say, 'When Auntie Kath asks you for a hug, she is asking for your consent or permission to hug you.' Ensure you child knows that they can expect all people to ask for their consent before entering their personal body boundary. For children who need ongoing medical assistance, discuss how healthcare professionals often need to enter their body boundary to help keep them well. However, reiterate that these healthcare workers still need to ask for consent and wait for a reply.

Pages 8-9

Review the two illustrations: Eli giving consent and not giving consent. Explain that giving consent is indicated by a happy or enthusiastic 'yes'. If a person says nothing or is unsure in any way by saying, 'I'm not sure', 'Maybe' or 'I don't know' then this not giving consent. Explain that consent can also be withdrawn at anytime and people can change their mind at anytime.

Pages 10-11

Ensure your child understands that people who are caring for them need to always 'check in'. They need to respect your child's voice. Ask, 'Does xxxx always check in with you to see if you are okay?' Reinforce that 'respect' is an important part of consent.

Pages 12-15

Ensure your child understands that they can greet people in any way they like. The person, who might be greeting your child, needs to ask how they would like to be greeted and/or if they would like, for example, a hug or a high-five as a greeting. Reiterate to your child that they also need to ask people how they would like to be greeted, or ask if they can give that person a hug or a kiss. And even if your child is non-verbal, people should never assume they can greet them in any way they like. Ask, 'If you said "yes" to a hug one day, do you have to agree to a hug the next day? Why is that?' Say, 'That's right because you can always change your mind.'

Pages 16-17

Unpack with your child the difference between private and public spaces. Ask, 'Do people knock on your door if they wish to enter your bedroom? What should all people do before entering a private space such as a bathroom or bedroom?' Reinforce the need for consent to be given when entering a private space and when dressing your child.

Pages 18-19

Discuss the word 'private' as meaning 'just for you'. Talk about private parts as those under our bathing suit (or underwear) and name them using the correct terms. *Note:* your child's mouth is also a private part, as are boys' nipples. Explain to your child that even though a boy's nipples are private, they are not covered by a bathing suit or underwear. For reasons why we encourage children to learn the correct names for their private parts go to: www.e2epublishing.info/blog/

Reiterate that it's okay for your child when they are alone, to touch their own private parts in a private space. *Note:* we never want our children to feel shame around the exploration of their private parts — which is all part of growing up.

Pages 20-21

Read this section carefully with your child and answer any questions they may have. Please take your time to unpack these pages. Ensure they understand points 1 and 2 on page 20. If your child needs help washing their private parts, make sure they understand that caregivers need to always ask for consent, and they (the child) have the right to say 'Stop!' at anytime if they feel uncomfortable or unsafe.

Pages 22-23

Reinforce that your child's mouth is a private part and dentists and doctors, or a caregiver cleaning your child's teeth must always ask for consent first.

Pages 24-27

Discuss with your child how their body is very smart and can let them know when they feel unsafe. Ask, 'What does your body do when you feel unsafe?' Say, 'What you are describing to me are your Early Warning Signs. This is your clever body letting you know you feel unsafe and that you need to tell a trusted adult straightaway.' Review the Early Warning Signs the child is experiencing on page 24. Say, 'Sometimes we might get only one or two of our Early Warning Signs, but sometimes we might get many of the signs this child is experiencing. Sometimes you might feel some of your Early Warning Signs because you are excited about doing something a little bit daring and scary like going on a ride at a fun park, and that's okay.' Ask, 'Have you ever felt a little bit scared in an exciting way? Where were you? What were you doing? How did your body tell you that you were excited, but a little bit scared at the same time? If you feel unsafe in a scared and frightened way, and your Early Warning Signs begin, what should you do? When have you felt your Early Warning Sings in an unsafe way?' Establish with your child who their safe adults are — these are adults that both you and your child trust. With your child, choose three to five adults to be on their Safety Network. *Note:* who your child chooses is their choice. Ensure one adult is not a family member. Your child will need to feel comfortable that these trusted adults will always believe them if they feel worried or unsafe.' (Review who a trusted adult is on page 25.) The adults on your child's Safety Network should also be accessible. Please ask them before writing their names on your child's safety hand. Make sure these trusted adults know it is an honor to be chosen, how important they are to your child and their role in your child's life. Display your child's safety hand in a prominent place. If you go to www.e2epublishing. info you will find a free safety hand to download or simply trace around your child's hand. At this point, you could also share a 'safety word' or 'safety sign'. This is a word or sign your child could indicate to an adult on their Safety Network, and that adult would know your child feels unsafe and the adult needs to act immediately. The word could be anything, for example, carrots, kangaroo or dinosaur; a sign could be thumbs down.

Pages 28-29

Review the list on page 28 that may make a child feel unsafe and need assistance from a trusted adult. Ask, 'Have you ever been yelled at or hit? Have you ever been spoken to in an unkind way? etc.' Ask your child about each point if appropriate to do so, and you know what to do if you **do** get a worrying disclosure. If the child does disclose or gives a worrying answer to your question/s, ensure you contact one of the key organizations listed in *Body Safety Education* or on our website. If there is a disclosure, stay calm — as your initial reaction is key to the child's ongoing health and healing. Reassure the child that:

• you believe them

• they have done the right thing in telling you

• they are incredibly brave and courageous

• they are in **no** way to blame

• they are safe and will be looked after

• you will do everything you can to stop the abuse, but make no promises.

Leave the child with a trusted adult and contact key organizations. Do not handle a disclosure on your own. *Note:* with more and more online grooming and abuse by people your child may know, ensure your child knows that no one (adult or child) should ask them to send pictures of their private parts. Practice saying the words on page 28 with your child. *Note:* it is totally understandable if a child feels too scared or frightened to tell the perpetrator to stop, but there is no harm in practicing these words when there is no threat. However, your child should always know if they ever feel unable to say or sign 'Stop!' in a real and threatening situation, the default is to always get away as soon as they can and tell a trusted adult on their Safety Network. Reiterate point 4 that any abuse is **never ever** a child's fault.

Pages 30-31

Review the safety procedures on page 30. Ask, 'What might you do if you can't find one of the people on your Safety Network?' Ensure your child knows that it is never too late to tell, and that you will always be there for them, and that you will always believe them. Be your child's 'safe person' — the person they can come to and tell anything to, and they will be believed.

Page 32-33

Ask, 'What do you think is the difference between a secret and a surprise? What should you do if someone asks you to keep a secret? Has anyone asked you to keep a secret that made you feel bad or uncomfortable? Has anyone asked you to keep a secret that made you experience your Early Warning Signs? What did you do?' *Note:* of course some children may need to tell a trusted adult about something that is worrying them, and they may not want others to know. A term you could use with your child in this kind of situation is 'private conversations'. These may refer to bodily changes such as puberty as they get older.

Pages 34-35

Discuss the meaning of 'rights'. Explain we all have them and children do too, and that rights are rules people need to follow. Please ensure all caregivers read this book (with or without your child) so they know your child's and your family's body safety rules they need to adhere to.

KEY TERMS

Body Boundary: the invisible personal space around your body and wheelchair

Consent: asking if something is okay or not okay; asking for and giving permission; saying or showing an enthusiastic 'yes' or saying or showing 'no'

Early Warning Signs: the physical things that happen to our body when we are worried, uncomfortable, scared or unsafe

Respect: understanding another person's wishes, treating them the way you want to be treated, and caring about them and their wishes

Safety Network: 3 to 5 safe and trusted adults that you could go to if you feel scared or worried, and they will listen, believe you and help you

Secrets: information that is often kept from others

Surprises: information that is most often happy and will always be told

Trust: belief in a person who wants the best for you and cares for you, and would never harm you

BOOKS BY THE SAME AUTHOR

Body Safety Education
A parents' guide to protecting kids from sexual abuse

This essential and easy-to-read guide contains simple, practical, and age-appropriate ideas on how parents, caregivers and educators can protect children from sexual abuse — ensuring they grow up as assertive and confident teenagers and adults.

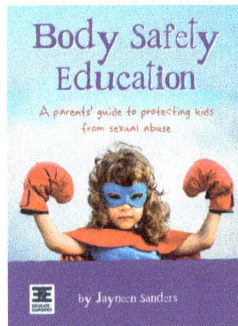

No Means No!

'No Means No!' is a children's picture book about an empowered little girl who has a very strong and clear voice in all issues, especially those relating to her body. This book teaches children about personal boundaries, respect, and consent; empowering kids by respecting their choices and their right to say, 'No!' Discussion Questions included. Suitable for children 2 to 9 years.

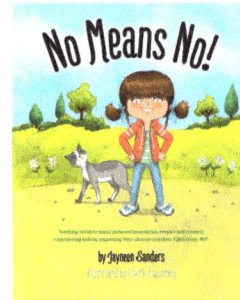

ABC of Body Safety and Consent

The 26 'key' letters and accompanying words and illustrations will help children to learn and consolidate crucial and life-changing body safety and consent skills. Discussion Questions included. Suitable for children 4 to 10 years.

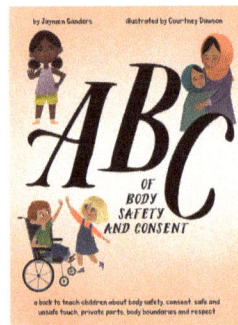

Some Secrets Should Never Be Kept

'Some Secrets Should Never Be Kept' is an award-winning and beautifully illustrated children's book that sensitively raises the subject of inappropriate touch. This book was written as a tool to help parents, caregivers, and teachers broach the subject with children in an age-appropriate and non-threatening way. Discussion Questions included. Suitable for children 3 to 11 years.

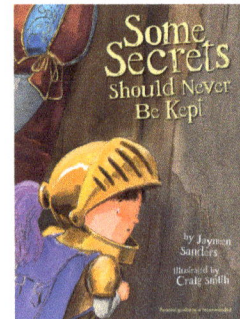

My Body! What I Say Goes!

A children's picture book to empower and teach children about personal body safety, feelings, safe and unsafe touch, private parts, secrets and surprises, consent and respect. Discussion Questions included. Ages 3 to 9 years.

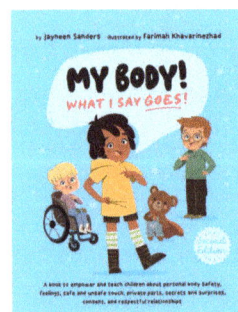

Let's Talk About Body Boundaries, Consent and Respect

Through familiar scenarios, this book opens up crucial conversations with children around consent and respect. A child growing up knowing they have a right to their own personal space, gives that child ownership and choices as to what happens to them. These concepts are presented in a child-friendly and easily-understood manner. Discussion Questions included. Suitable for children 4 to 10 years.

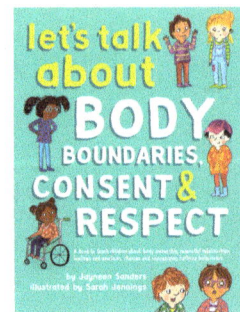

My Body! What I Say Goes! Kiah's Edition

A children's body safety book designed specifically for First Nations' children and illustrated by awarded-winning Indigenous artist and Dharug woman, Jasmine Seymour. Topics covered: feelings, safe and unsafe touch, private parts, secrets and surprises and consent. Discussion Questions included. Ages 3 to 9 years.

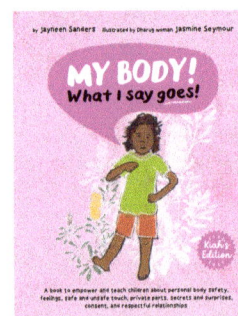

for more books and free resources go to www.e2epublishing.info

www.ingramcontent.com/pod-product-compliance
Lightning Source LLC
Chambersburg PA
CBHW041635040426

42448CB00021B/3486